LIFE AFTER PRISON

LIFE AFTER PRISON

Al Wengerd

HERALD PRESS
Scottdale, Pennsylvania
Waterloo, Ontario

The paper used in this publication is recycled and meets the minimum requirements of American National Standard of Information Sciences—Permanence of Paper for Printed Library Materials, ANSI Z39.48-1984.

TABLE OF CONTENTS

A Personal Word to You. . .

This little booklet is written to you, a prisoner. Although people have written about prisons and prisoners endlessly, I hope this booklet is different. I want to write to you and not about you. I want to write for you and not for other folks.

This booklet is not the result of a survey. It is not scientific. Some of it may not even be true. During the past years I have walked and sat with friends and listened as they talked about leaving the joint and going home. I am writing this now to try to share with you some of the things I have learned during all of this. I feel like maybe it's a kind of mirror that I can hold up for you to take a look at yourself. What do you see? Although all of you are different, you will also all see some things that are the same.

I've never been a prisoner. I'm not proud or ashamed of that. But many of my friends have been prisoners and I guess that's my main qualification. I've seen them suffer while in prison and also after they got out. I've thought that maybe, if they had had something like this, it could have made things just a bit easier. My other qualification is that all of us are more alike than we are different. Our friends, our families, our goals in life are about the same. I have thought of this often while I was writing.

ON THE STREET

Chapter 1

Surviving on the street is different from surviving inside. It takes thinking and planning about where to stay and how to get a job. It means meeting people who don't understand where you've been. It means keeping your cool when others bait you. It means taking responsibility for yourself and taking control of your life.

TERRY: "I'm broke."

The phone rang. "Hello."
"Can you come and get me?"
"Is this you, Terry?"
"Yeah, I just got out yesterday."
"Well, yeah, I can come and get you. Where are you?"
"The bus station."
"Okay, I'll see you in about an hour."
We meet. "Have you had breakfast yet?"
"No."
"Let's get some."
"I'm broke."
"That's okay, I'll buy."
"Wow, this is weird eating this stuff—it's food!"
"Say Terry, where'd you spend the night?"
"Well, I missed my bus in Indianapolis so I had to wait all night for the next one."
"You stayed in the bus terminal all night?"
"Yeah."
"That's a pretty tough way to start. Where are you going to stay now that you're out?"
"I don't know—I guess I'll have to find a place."

THE PROBLEM:

Terry didn't have a plan. He only had a day to get it together. He had no money and no place to go.

Not all exits from prison are as sudden as Terry's. You will probably have a couple of weeks from the time the "ticket" arrives until the gate opens. Still, you may not be any more prepared than Terry was. I'm sure you've thought about how you'll spend that first day, where you'll spend that first night. Wild, isn't it? Maybe, but maybe not. Maybe you'll feel more like easing into it. It's like when you go to the beach and the water feels so cold—some slide in slowly while others dive in head first.

SOME IDEAS AND SUGGESTIONS:

Whether you will ease back into your situation or come crashing home may depend on how you think about it ahead of time and whether or not you've made some plans. Here are some things to consider.

1) Planning your own life is going to be a new experience. You've been in a place where most of your decisions were made for you. You've been told where to go, what to do, when to do it and—you know the rest. Even if you have wanted to take control of your own life, about the most you could do was decide how to use your commisary or how to pay off a gambling debt. It will take awhile to get used to making your own plans and choices.

2) I think there's a difference between planning and dreaming. Dreaming can be a way of shutting out reality while planning can be a way of taking hold of your situation and making it work for you. Planning means picking and choosing between things that are real possibilities for you. An example would be trying to decide whether it's best to live with your mother or your grandmother. Both may be possibilities. Which would be best?

3) Plans usually involve other people. Don't assume that you know what other people are thinking or that you can make plans for them. If you are thinking about living with your mother or your grandmother, check out your idea with them before you arrive at their doorsteps. Do you fit into their plans? Will you have a ride? Is somebody going to be there the day you get out? Do you have a back-up plan if your first one doesn't work?

4) It's nice to have some money when you come home. You probably won't have too much when you leave so what you do with it is pretty important. It's important to have some money for your first Big Mac, for a flower for your Mom. And those state shoes—you'll need a pair of *real* shoes now!

---

1. How are you going to feel wearing all your own clothes again? What if they are out of style? What if they don't fit? What if your tastes have changed?

2. Do you want to leave a few bucks for a friend who is really having it tough? Or, would it be better to keep your money for now and send him some after you get a job?

GEORGE: "I'm scared."

"I'm scared, man I'm shaken!"
"What do you mean, you're scared?"
"I haven't done a darn thing for two years. I haven't had to worry about anything—no responsibility. I think I can do it, but I don't know. I have a place to stay—I'm living with Karen's folks. And I have a job. Things are working out a lot better than I thought; I guess the man upstairs is looking after me."
"Yeah, I'd say so."
"But I'm still scared."

THE PROBLEM:

It took me by surprise. Why was he scared? He was in only two years, had a family that cared, good job skills and a job—even some money in the bank! What more did he want? As we continued to talk I began to realize that thinking ahead and planning couldn't get rid of the fear. George wasn't scared about being able to work or having enough money. He was scared about how to act, how he would respond to those first glances from family, from friends, from employers and fellow-workers. This was new stuff for George; he had never been an "ex-con" before.

And that's the way some people will react to you. You'll think real hard before you fill in the job application space that asks about your last job. There are many possible answers: "I worked for the state; I was unemployed; I was self-employed (hustling); I was in school; I was in prison." It will always be a tough question.

SOME IDEAS AND SUGGESTIONS:

George's fears were pretty normal and you're likely to experience some of the same fears. And that's okay—fear isn't bad. It's a natural part of a new experience and even good planning probably won't get rid of it completely. The best thing is to accept that the fear is there and then work at ways to handle that fear.

1) Work at being as honest as you can with people. You don't have to wear a sign that says "I just got out of prison." But you could work at leveling with as many people as possible. Don't go out of your way to bring it up, but if it comes up, you can say "I made a mistake and I paid for it. For me, it's over and done with." Most people can accept that and accept you.

11

The situation can be more sticky, though, when family members have been covering for you. Suppose your mother has told a friend that you've been working in the oil fields in Louisiana while you were gone; now this friend is coming to visit. What now? Can you tell the truth without embarassing your mother? How? Are there other solutions?

2) Try to have at least one other person in your life that you can talk to about your experience. It could be a friend or a sympathetic minister, *somebody* who's willing to listen and help you with questions when you're struggling. Parole officers are often not the best listeners—even when they care about you they usually don't have that kind of time. There may also be some organizations in your area that could help. Ask your counselor or chaplain.

3) Whatever you do, don't deny your fears! Whether they're big or little, they're real and they need to be taken seriously. Some people need to talk about their fears—others just need quiet. You may find comfort and healing through your faith in God. Spend time in daily prayer—ask God to guide you and watch over you.

---

1. Do you want to tell people you're getting out? Who do you want to tell? Why?

2. How long will it take until you feel like you're really home, settled in? How long till you quit feeling like an ''ex-con?''

BOBBY: ''I blew it!''

''I don't know why I hit him. After it was all over I realized it wasn't necessary. It was a dumb thing to do. I guess I thought I was still in the joint. All he did was say something about the lady I was with and I lost my cool. I could have walked out. I didn't have to stay there. You'd think that after two years I'd be over it. I guess those 17 years in the joint did something to me. I didn't realize until later why I reacted that way.''

THE PROBLEM:

Bobby spent 17 years in prison and he survived. Surviving inside meant never being caught off-guard, never looking weak, always saving face. One mistake could mean his reputation and freedom, or even his life. He didn't take nothing from nobody!

After two years on the street Bobby knew that he didn't have to react that way anymore and he thought he had it under control. But prison reactions are hard to unlearn and when somebody insulted his girlfriend he lost his cool. He couldn't believe he did it—he knew he couldn't let it happen again. So we talked, talked about how he could have responded differently or even avoided the situation.

SOME IDEAS AND SUGGESTIONS:

You may not have experienced prison as violently as Bobby did. You may also not be the kind of person who handles his problems by fighting. Still, you probably were forced into situations where you needed to save face. And now, when you're getting out, it may be helpful to try to think about different ways you could respond when somebody challenges you.

1) Try to avoid places where you think people may confront you. Maybe that means not going to the local bar or club. At least for the first while, avoid going into places where you are likely to be challenged.

2) Learn to walk away from situations. Even if you are careful about where you go you may run into somebody who wants to set you up. In prison you probably didn't walk away—that might have made you look weak. But I think it's different on the street. Out there you can say, "This isn't worth it. I don't have to show them that I can get in the last lick. I have a choice—I can walk away and forget it."

3) You may have to learn to side-step confrontations on the job. Other workers, if they find out that you've been in prison, may make fun of you and put you down. When it's taken you a long time to get a job you can't really afford to get in a fight or even to walk away completely. So what are you going to do? Are you going to keep your anger inside and let it out later, maybe at your family? Can you take the sting out of the situation by being straight with your co-workers? Is there any humor in the situation that could help to reduce the tension when they first find out? Could you level with your supervisor and request a transfer to another department? If the harassment continues, at what point do you just give up and quit? These are some of the choices you may have to make.

4) Keep your head clear. People always make better judgments when they are not drinking or doing drugs. That was part of Bobby's problem. He knew he shouldn't drink but thought he just had to try it. And, he blew it. How about you?

1. Do you know what sets you off most easily? Comments about yourself or about your girlfriend? Your family? Comments about your past or your race?

2. What places in your town are you most likely to run into trouble? Will you need to go there to prove that you can handle it? Or could you just let those places go with the rest of your past?

3. How did crowds affect you before you were in prison? Does that have anything to do with why you went to prison?

ON THE JOB

Chapter 2

Part of surviving on the street is the whole thing of getting and keeping a job. Sometimes jobs are hard to find and you may have to take one you don't really care for. Once you're hired you have to prove that you have the physical strength and/or skills required to do the job right. You have to be able to take orders. All of these things are part of taking charge of your own life.

TOM: "I can't find a job."

"Shoot, I can't find a job. There just aren't any out there. I mean, I've looked *everywhere!* I just came from the employment office. The same old story. 'Sorry, Mr. Miller, we don't have anything today.' It's been two weeks—you'd think I'd be able to find something, but no, not me. How do they expect you to get started? It's a trap—always the same. 'Do you have your own transportation? How about a driver's license?' 'No, no I don't.' 'Well then, I'm sorry, we can't hire you.' No car, no job. How am I supposed to get wheels without a job?"

THE PROBLEM:

It's a familiar story. It's also a discouraging story for a lot of guys getting out. After all, $70 sure won't buy a car these days!

But maybe Tom's situation isn't as hopeless as he thinks. Let's check out more carefully some of the things he just said:

"I've looked everywhere." We all know that that's probably not true, though Tom probably *felt* like he had looked everywhere. Looking everywhere in two weeks would have taken some pretty fast walking. Tom probably really meant that right now he simply couldn't think of any other places to check.

"No, not me." Tom seemed to be thinking that he was the only one without a job. He was so busy feeling sorry for himself he probably forgot to notice the lines of people at the employment office. Although I never saw Tom walk into a place to ask for a job, I imagine him walking in slowly, shuffling his feet, as if to say, "You don't have a job for me either, do you?"

"It's a trap." Tom sounds about ready to give up because he thinks all jobs will require him to have a car and he can't get a car until he

has a job. But *do* all jobs need a car? For some companies it may be the deciding factor. Others really just want the employee to show up ready to work.

SOME IDEAS AND SUGGESTIONS:

Getting a job is Number 1 when it comes down to making it on your own. It takes a job to be as independent as you want to be and to get the things you've been wanting for a long time. A job will also help you manage your time by giving some shape to your days. A few guys I've known have had jobs waiting for them when they got out. Most of them aren't so lucky. Just finding a job can be a big job. Here are some things Tom found helpful, both in finding places that were hiring and in getting himself hired.

1) Take a look at yourself in the mirror before you leave the house. Do you look like somebody *you* would hire? If you look and act like a loser when you're checking on a job, chances are you won't get hired. So you've got to look like you care about yourself. That doesn't mean getting a three-piece suit or even a new pair of Levis. Some simple things will help. Be clean. Be neat. Wear the clothes you expect to work in. If you are hoping to get a factory job, wear work clothes. If you are applying for a supervisor's job, dress accordingly.

2) Not too many guys get jobs through the state employment offices. It's still useful to register with them and check in now and then. But your best bet lies with other people who are employed. Check with your family and friends who are working. Ask them to pick up application forms for you. Most job openings never get to the employment office or the newspaper ads, the two places where most people begin their job hunting. It's basically like the grapevine where you are now—other employees are the first to know when there is an opening. So if you're serious about getting a job, stay in touch with the folks who are working.

3) Be persistent. If you know that a company is going to be hiring soon, go there every *morning*, not in the afternoon. That shows you're motivated. You don't have to take a lot of their time, just let them see you, *often!* It's a lot like getting your counselor to do something for you. Don't be a nuisance and make them mad at you, but do show them that you are serious. You are not just out for the exercise.

4) Use your afternoons to take care of all the little things that need to be done after you get out. During those first weeks you will need to spend your mornings looking for work. But in the afternoons you

18

need to do things like getting your driver's license; you probably won't be able to do that without taking off work once you're hired. Make sure you have a social security card. You can apply for a duplicate card at the local social security office. Also very important —make sure that you can be easily reached by phone, either your own or a friendly neighbor's. Lots of employers just won't bother hiring you if they can't get you by phone.

5) Demonstrate a teachable attitude. In other words, don't be a know-it-all. Your willingness to learn is as important as the skills you bring to the job. Even a familiar job may have changed while you were gone, so be ready to listen.

6) Don't be too picky about the kind of job or the hours you're willing to work. Sometimes you may have to settle for what you don't really like: bad hours, too few hours, poor pay or fringe benefits, work that really doesn't suit you. When the job market is tight it helps to remember that most people probably don't find their jobs ideal. It also helps to remember that you don't have to stick with a job for the rest of your life, though you probably also shouldn't plan to be changing too often.

---

1. Should you check with the local unions when looking for a job?

2. Are you willing to accept a job that you won't be able to take for very long just so you'll have a few bucks to help you get on your feet?

3. Do you remember the dates and the names of places you worked at before?

SAM: "I got a job."

"Dad, it's for you."
"Hello, this is Al."
"Hey, I got a job. I start tomorrow."
"Great! Do you have a ride?"
"Yeah, I'll ride with Bill and another guy."
"Sounds great! Let me know how it's going."

(A week later) "Al, I just got fired."
"You did? Why?"
"I guess I wasn't working fast enough."

"Did you miss any work?"

"We were late once but we called in so it was okay."

"I'm sorry—I don't know what else to say."

THE PROBLEM:

"All that time spent looking for work right down the drain! Failed again! What's a guy to do when the best he can do isn't good enough? The heck with it! I don't have to take this!"

This is the way I *expected* Sam to react. But he didn't. He made some other choices. He decided that he was going right back there and ask this guy again why he fired him. Now that takes guts!

But it was worth it. After Sam told him how much he needed the job and how hard he had tried to do his best, the foreman had a change of heart; he hired Sam back and gave him a 50c raise!

· SOME IDEAS AND SUGGESTIONS:

There's no way to guarantee that you'll ever have a foreman like Sam had, somebody who's willing to give you another chance. Even so, Sam's approach could still be useful for you and it sure beats giving up!

1) Remember that not all job problems are your fault. Apparently Sam's boss was having a bad day on Friday and he took it out on Sam. You know what that's like. All bosses have good days and bad days, just like you. So sometimes you also have to be willing to give the boss a second chance.

2) You don't have to accept an impulsive answer as the *final* answer. Sam didn't argue with the boss, cuss him out, throw things and walk out the door. He kept his cool. He gave his boss time to cool off over the weekend and then went back and talked to him. If he had thrown a fit on Friday the boss would probably have refused to see him on Monday.

3) Sometimes your best *won't* be good enough. Sam really hadn't *worked* in three years and he knew he was soft. He knew that he'd be dragging after the first day, that he wouldn't be able to do as much as some of the other guys. But he didn't give up because he knew it would get better.

4) You may want to consider doing some things Sam *didn't* do. Maybe you could begin exercising when you get out, or even before.

Maybe you could start to get back in shape by getting rid of some of the pounds you put on eating the stuff they call food in prison. Or, you could offer to work for a slightly lower wage for the first few weeks, until you've shown that you can keep up with the others. Should you tell the foreman where you've been? Or does he know already? Does he understand? How you handle this situation depends on what kind of person your boss is as well as on you.

In the end, even if you do all of these things, you may still find, on your first job, that your best isn't good enough. Accept it, if you can't get a second chance, and go on. Chances are pretty good, you'll do better on your next job.

---

1. Do you know when to leave the situation as it is and go on to something else or when to ask for another chance?

2. If you haven't been doing hard physical work for awhile, are there ways you can get yourself ready for that?

3. Which is most important, being physically ready for a job or mentally ready?

WILLIE: "I don't have to take orders."

"It's been awhile now and I can do it. But when I first started working there, I couldn't. Whenever someone told me to do something, I'd challenge it. Every time. I couldn't take orders. Then a friend told me, 'Willie, you got to cool it. You'll get fired!'
'Why? What did I do?'
'The foreman's getting upset. No matter what he tells you to do, you bitch.' I was glad I had a friend there who knew me. I'm sure I wouldn't have lasted three weeks if I hadn't. You know, I spent 10 years hating it every time they told me what to do. I'm a man! Men don't take orders! They give them!"

THE PROBLEM:

Willie told me later that he lost track of how many times he had to go back to the foreman to apologize.

After 10 years of living under an authority that often abused him, Willie wanted none of it! That's why he couldn't take direction from

21

the foreman—the foreman represented the authority he thought he had left behind when he hit the street.

Authority—what's the first thing that comes to your mind when you hear that word? The cop who busted you, the judge who gave you time, the sergeant on second shift?

Most people in prison have experienced some abuse of authority. Police brutality is real. Courts do discriminate. Prisons are not run fairly. *You* know who gets the breaks. Too often it's not those who deserve them but those who can afford them. Or those who can play the system.

Now it's time to get out. Time to go home. And maybe time to have some new ideas about what authority means. Is there anything good about it? Can you ever get to the point where you can accept authority and feel okay about it? For many people who have been in prison the answer is "No!" They used to think the world was fair—now they don't. They used to think our court system honored truth—now they know that's not always the case. They thought all criminal justice personnel were there to help them—now they know better. And in prison, it's important to know these things—you have to know them in order to make sense of the prison world. But will they help you make sense of the world outside? Or will they get you in trouble?

For Willie, it meant trouble. He had forgotten that giving and taking orders is what makes most businesses run. Instead, he was reminded of where he had been and he didn't like that one bit.

SOME IDEAS AND SUGGESTIONS:

Changing old attitudes is not easy. You can't just leave your attitudes behind the way you leave your stamps for a friend. So it will be helpful if you have some ideas of what you can do when it is tough to take orders.

1) Be willing to admit your mistake when you go off on somebody who tells you what to do. Don't be afraid to say, "I think maybe I was wrong." Men and women both *do* give orders but they also both take them.

2) People around you are taking orders, too. Sometimes it's easy to feel like the boss is just picking on you—he isn't telling *others* what to do all the time. Maybe that's true. But before you act on that feeling, check it out. For example, if you were the last person hired you may have to be willing to take instructions from several other

people who have been there longer. Or suppose you're not a machine operator—your job is to supply the line. There is a difference between these two jobs and it may mean that you have to take more orders than the machine operator.

3) Taking orders does not make you less of a person, regardless of whether you are a man or a woman. There is dignity in doing honest work and doing it well—taking orders sometimes means that you can be a part of a team that creates something worthwhile. Although businesses don't always recognize it, they are depending on the work of each employee to produce a good product. And, whether it's recognized or not, nobody can take away your personal satisfaction when you do *your* part well.

4) Orders are bad only when they are given to insult you as a person, to cut you down. It is not unreasonable for somebody to tell you to open the door for the tow motor. However, it may be a putdown when another worker tells you to go to the lunch room to get his lunch bucket for him. If this should happen, you might say, ''Is this to be a regular part of my job?'' Few people will say ''Yes.'' He'll get the picture. If it persists, talk to *his* boss. Of course, it gets more complicated if you are being hassled by the owner of the business.

5) It is impossible to avoid all authority. All your relationships with others involve people who have some kind of a claim on you. It means you are somehow responsible to them—they have some kind of authority over you. This includes your boss, your parents, your wife, even your landlord. At some point they may all have reason to tell you what to do—they all have some say about your life. Can you hear them and do what they want? Can you choose which requests are reasonable and which are for the birds? Can you say no to a request without blowing up? These situations will take all the self-control and clear-thinking you can muster.

---

1. How would you handle authority over others at work?

2. How will you react the first time you are pulled over for speeding? What will you say when your parole officer questions what you tell him? Or the first time he denies you a travel pass to go see your aunt?

IN THE FAMILY

Chapter 3

Learning how to make it on the street and on the job is necessary for your survival, your physical survival. There are other kinds of survival, survival that has to do with the part of you that nobody can see. It's called emotional survival, survival of your soul, of your spirit. This survival probably involves others who are important to you like your family, your wife and kids, your girlfriend. How well this invisible part of you survives depends a lot on how well all of you fit back together after you come home. All of you have changed while you've been gone and it is not possible to go back to the way things were before. Maybe you wouldn't even want that. You will all need to accept each other where you are now and see if you can develop new, and maybe better, relationships as husband and wife, as lovers, as parents and children.

DAN: "I'm powerless."

"I asked her about the baby and she said it had died. I felt helpless, full of anger. I wasn't there to help—that's why it happened. Then I told her 'Don't leave me, you're all I've got.' She was silent. I knew something was wrong. 'Is there somebody else?' She didn't say anything. I knew. What could I do? It wasn't her fault I was away. I knew it could happen. I was afraid it *would* happen. I felt absolutely powerless. My bones ached. I was weak.

"Then I woke up in a cold sweat. It was only a dream. Thank God, it was only a dream!"

THE PROBLEM:

Being in prison is risky business. It threatens families and marriages and other love relationships. Dan knew that—he had thought about that and now his fears were coming to him in a dream. He was glad that it *was* a dream—some of his friends were not so lucky.

Now that you're getting ready to go home you may be seeing problems in your family and tensions in your marriage, problems and tensions you never felt before. You may be having questions. Does your wife really want you back? What if she's involved with someone else and she hasn't told you because she doesn't want to hurt you?

SOME IDEAS AND SUGGESTIONS:

All people who care about each other have problems. Always remember that. And after what you and your family have just been going through, you're entitled to some larger problems. They're nothing to be ashamed of, just something to work with.

1) Don't deny problems in your family. That's what some people do, no matter how much evidence there is pointing to the problem. Think about your wife and family — have any of them given you any signals that they're expecting any kind of problems after you get home?

2) Don't go looking for trouble. This is the opposite of #1. Some people, instead of denying all problems, are actually looking for them. They are always testing to see if their families still accept them or love them. Do you doubt your wife when she tells you where she was last Friday night? Does she have to spend a lot of time in every letter telling you that she still loves you? What if she forgets something you asked her to do? Do you think that's a sign she doesn't love you anymore?

3) It will take some time to rebuild trust and confidence between you and your wife, between you and your children. Try to remember that in your present setting the level of trust is very low. There are probably very few, if any, people you really trust. So, for awhile it will be hard to trust your family just because you're not used to trusting people. It may be even harder when you realize how much you really need them. You may feel that life would be really hopeless without them. However, that's only partly right — life would be very painful and difficult without them but it would probably not be hopeless.

4) Don't be afraid to get help. Sometimes that may just mean talking to a friend. Other times it may mean getting some professional counseling for both you and your family. The adjustment to being a family again is a big one — don't be afraid to work at it very seriously.

---

1. What is the best response to a "Dear John" letter just before you come home? Do you just give up? If there are children involved, what is your responsibility to them?

2. How do you get back the control of your life that has been so completely taken away from you while you are in prison?

3. If you're going home to live with one or both of your parents, have you asked them exactly how long you can stay? A week? A month? As long as you need to?

BUBBA: "What happened to my kids?"

"If I have to tell you kids again, I'm going to beat your butts. . . Boy, I don't know what you did to these kids while I was gone but they sure changed! I might as well talk to that chair over there. Did you see that, when he walked out of the room? He looked at me like he was saying 'Who do you think *you* are?' I got to teach these kids some respect! You must have let them do whatever they wanted! What's for supper?"

THE PROBLEM:

Bubba has come home and has met his children. He assumes that their mother has been too easy on them while he was away and that he can get things back under control by being tough with the kids.

This situation is repeated over and over. While you're away Mom is in control. She's *had* to be—there wasn't anybody else. So when you get back you can't understand why the kids don't respect you, don't listen to you. Even if they're not *your* children they ought to respect your authority. Maybe you've even thought that's what *she* wanted—for you to come home and straighten up these kids.

SOME IDEAS AND SUGGESTIONS:
Kids are tough. You can't beat them into being good. If you try to do that, they'll only get worse in the end. Respect is earned, not demanded. Think about where you are now. Do you respect anybody in authority? If so, is it because you're afraid of them or because you think they care about you, at least a little? Think about that when you get to know your kids again.

1) Be prepared for changes. Bubba wasn't—he thought things would be just like they always were. But they weren't and they won't be for you, either. The longer you've been gone, the greater the changes. It's not that you haven't been a good parent, just an *absent* parent. Your kids learned to survive without you. Now that you're back, it will take awhile for them to adjust. The key is time—you may need to give it a couple of months, or even more.

29

2) Kids go through stages—they are changing all the time. So go easy on yourself—not all the changes you see in them have been caused by your being gone. If your kids are between the ages of 12 and 16, chances are they would be rebellious even if you *had* been at home. Do you remember what you were like at that age? It might help to talk to a friend who has kids about the same age as yours. Are your kids *really* that different? If you think they are, it might be a good idea to get some help. Counseling for families is often a good way to understand what's happening to each person in the family.

3) Parents need to understand that kids can have bad days, too. Try not to over-react to occasional bad behavior. If your kid *never* listens to you, you've got a serious problem. If he occasionally doesn't listen, that's another matter. Nobody ever said your kids were going to be perfect.

4) Always remember the difference between respect and fear. We all want respect—we all *need* respect. And we need it especially from those we love. You may be tempted to take the short cut and use fear to get it. That's the way it's done in the joint. But that's not what you want for people you love. Respect is like an opening flower. You can't pick it up and shake it and expect it to open up in full bloom. It won't work. Even if you watch a flower every day, you may not notice it opening, until one day, WOW, it's there!

5) Don't let the way you discipline the children get between you and your partner. Bubba was ready to blame it all on his wife—it made him feel needed. But was that helpful? It may take a long time to work this out and it will probably *never* be exactly the way it was before. Maybe your wife has learned that sometimes she can handle them better than you and she may not be ready to give that up. This can be one of the toughest problems you'll have to face. Talk about it. Be ready to compromise, to work out a new balance of authority and discipline between the two of you.

6) You and your children will both be affected by the way other people respond to them. What will your kids' friends say the first time they come to your house after you're home? Do their parents know you've been in prison? Will the other parents allow their kids to continue the friendship? How your kids feel about you may depend partly on how their friends treat them after you're home.

---

1. What do you do when it looks like your kids are becoming too much like you? We all face that. I'm a perfectionist. And my nine-year-old son? You're right—just like his old man! Maybe I'll have to change me before I can expect to help him change.

2. Maybe you got married since you're in the joint. What do you expect from her children? Have you talked about it?

3. Does it make a difference if they aren't your kids? Can you be a family even when you and your lover aren't married?

JULIE: "He's not the same."

"That's all we used to talk about. What it was going to be like when he came home. Making love. Going for walks. Waking up in the middle of the night and having him there. . . He used to be so sensitive, so tender. . . Now. . .I don't know. I can't say exactly. It's like part of him still hasn't gotten out. Sometimes I look at him when the TV is on and he's just kind of staring into space. I don't know what's going on inside of him. Doesn't he love me anymore?"

THE PROBLEM:

Julie knows it, she feels it. Their marriage is being stretched. But her husband isn't the only one who's changed—*Julie* has changed too. They were both hoping it would be the same. Maybe someday, but for now it looks like it will be different. Whose fault is it?

Hers: Should she have written more often? Visited more often? Maybe she should have moved closer to the prison so she could be in closer contact. Is he upset because she's going to church?

His: He is the one that left. He could have written more, too, etc.

We could go on with this list but it probably wouldn't help. Probably neither Julie or her husband is to blame for what they are feeling. Both have changed, not necessarily because they *wanted* to but because they *had* to in order to survive. She needed to become more independent. He needed to become more <u>de</u>pendent. She may have become more affectionate with the children. He may have become *less* affectionate so that it wouldn't hurt so much to say goodbye. This list of changes could go on and on.

Does he love her any less? Probably not. Dealing with changes is hard when you don't understand them. It's even harder when you don't even know that they have happened. So it's helpful when you can name a change that has happened. It gives you a chance to try to understand how that change may affect your life now.

1) Prison is a tough place to survive emotionally. In order to survive you may have chosen to withdraw while you were there. You haven't made more than one or two friends. You act cold. It's a reasonable way to go. You might crack up if you didn't. But what does that do to you as a person? When you turn off your feelings like that, can you expect to turn them back on the day you walk out? Can you start trusting people that same afternoon? You may find that you'll need to take some risks when you start trusting others the way you'd like. Take it slowly knowing that you will sometimes also get hurt out here.

2) Being close to people is scary after you've been in prison for awhile. Julie wanted to be close, to feel close. She had waited for that for a long time. And now she still didn't feel close because being close scared her husband. I've seen guys simply disappear after being out only a week or so. Sometimes being around family and friends was just too much of a shock after having been in prison. Most guys come back after they've had a little time, a little space. How do you think you'll respond when people want to get close to you?

3) It will take time to adjust to physical contact with others, both sexual and otherwise. What will you do when your friend gives you a big hug? Will you pull away when others reach out to touch you? It may make you uncomfortable, especially since you've been in a joint where guys don't touch each other unless they are coming on. And, as long as you've waited to be with your woman, don't rush now. It may take some time, some getting to know each other again, before you can both really relax with each other. Will you be able to give yourself, *and* her, the time you both need to reestablish this intimate relationship?

4) Some of the changes that happen when you're in prison can help you grow. Often wives who are forced to make it on their own find that they are strong people who can take care of themselves when they have to. This may have happened to your wife and it may mean that you will have to grow, too. It takes a big person to accept and encourage growth and independence in someone who has depended on you in the past. Again, talk about it. You will need to work out a new balance here, too, so that you can both respect each other as equal partners.

1. Who will manage the money now that you're home?

2. Has she moved? What if the new place doesn't feel like home to you or you don't like the neighborhood?

3. How will you feel when she goes to work every morning and you sit at home with no job? Could you do some of the work around the house so she wouldn't have to do that, too, when she gets home?

INSIDE OF YOU

Chapter 4

I've been talking to you about a lot of changes, changes that have happened already because you've been in prison and changes that you can expect after you get out. Some of the changes are outside of you—they involve people and situations on the street, on the job and in your family. Some of the changes are inside of you. These inside changes are related to outside changes—how you are doing inside affects how well you get on outside. How you feel about yourself affects how you get along with others. It always helps to understand what's happening inside of yourself. Understanding yourself can bring you to a point of desiring forgiveness. Being able to forgive yourself, accepting God's forgiveness and possibly that of the victim can all be important steps in your inner changes.

RAY: "Leave me alone."

"Just leave me alone. When I get out of here I don't want nobody to pick me up. I just wanna be by myself. I'll stop at every restaurant on the way home. I wanna stop wherever I want to. Take any way home I want. I'm so sick of being around people. You can't ever be alone in this place. No matter where you go, what you do, there's always somebody looking. Twenty times an hour somebody walks by and looks in your cell. Sometimes I feel like screaming, like sticking somebody just for looking!"

THE PROBLEM:

Ray desperately needs some time for himself, some personal space. That by itself is not a problem. It becomes a problem when he, and others, don't understand or accept that he needs to be alone, at least for awhile when he first gets out. If this is how you feel it can be pretty tough on your family. They have waited a long time to be near you again—they want to be able to grab you and hug you and never let you go. So, will they understand that when you want to be by yourself it doesn't mean that you don't love them anymore? Will you be able to accept and understand that about yourself?

The need to be alone is pretty normal after being in prison for awhile. Prison is a lonely place because you're away from those you love and you're scared to get too close to those around you. And there are lots of people around you; you are never alone, just lonely. You can get to feeling that if one more person talks to you, you'll explode! It's the same feeling that keeps you in your cell or your dorm instead of going to the mess hall for dinner, grabbing those few precious moments when it may be quiet, moments when maybe you can write a letter or work on some craft without somebody looking over your shoulder.

This need to be alone is like a hunger. It may take awhile for you to get enough. Will you be able to explain to your family that you need to spend some time alone? Will they understand if you want to go for a long walk or maybe spend a couple of days somewhere by yourself? Or, you may want to spend the first days or week at home with just your family or closest friends. You may not feel like going to the store. You may not want to see a movie or even go out to eat. Can you explain it to them so they'll understand?

SOME IDEAS AND SUGGESTIONS:

Needing to be alone may be a good sign. It means you probably have resisted letting others control your life totally. It may mean that you haven't allowed others to make every decision for you and that you are eager to take charge of your own life again. So accept your need to be alone—it is probably a necessary stopping point along the way to complete freedom.

1) Try to balance *your* need to be alone with your family and friends' needs to show their love and acceptance. You may have to push yourself some and be with people more than you'd like. Hopefully this won't always be the case but during your first several weeks or months it may be difficult.

2) Let others know how you feel. It is probably better to give a direct answer like "No, I don't want to do that," than to make up some excuse. Explain to them your need to be alone as well as you can. And, even if they don't understand completely, ask them to be patient with you while you adjust.

3) Don't try to avoid crowds altogether. I remember one person who would get very upset when he was in a crowded place. He later realized that it was probably because it reminded him of where he had been. He sometimes misinterpreted people who wanted to be close to him. Even when they just wanted to show their support and love for him, he just couldn't take it. Eventually, though, he learned to accept their wanting to be next to him and now he really appreciates it.

38

1. *Do you think you'll be ready to start work as soon as you get home? Would it be better to take a week or so to sort of ease into tight places?*

2. *What if you still want to be alone a lot after you've been out a few months? Should you give yourself some more time? Would you feel okay about getting help?*

SONNY: "Victim? Yeah, I care."

"I hear you. Like, I thought about it while I was in the county jail. But now I don't know. Does it make any sense—going to prison and then paying restitution?"

"Maybe it's more than restitution. What about saying you're sorry? That is, if you are."

"I am, I am. I've thought about this now that I'm getting out. You know, they just live around the corner from my folks. I guess I just hoped I wouldn't run into them. Not that I'd *do* anything, but you know, what could I say? I mean I *want* to make it right. That's what I'd want if someone ripped me off."

THE PROBLEM:

While not everybody in prison is guilty, most people are. Sonny knew that *he* was guilty—he knew that he was responsible for what had happened. But now that he was getting ready to go home, he didn't know what to do with that responsibility. He knew that he had "paid" for his crime. Did his responsibility to the victim, and to himself, mean more than doing time?

I've found that most people feel bad about what they did before they even land in the joint. That may surprise some but I bet it doesn't surprise you. Some people would give anything to be able to undo what happened. Often that's impossible, but not always. While they can't actually undo a crime, like it never happened, they can sometimes mend the situation in the same way that a broken leg is mended when it heals.

You have to take your victim pretty seriously to be able to work at this. Some guys think their victims deserved what they got. Others think they must have forgotten by now. Still others think that all victims want is to see the offender locked up for a long time. These things are true sometimes but not always. My experience with victims tells me that often victims are not like that—it always depends on what happened in each particular case.

Victims are often ignored after the first police report is taken. Your victims probably don't know what happened to you. If they do know anything, it's probably only what they read in the paper. They don't know about your family, your alcohol problem, your childhood, when or how long you've been locked up, all the things you've accomplished since you've been locked up, etc.

The idea of getting back in touch with your victims may be pretty scary to you. At the same time, it might be helpful for all of you. Maybe you wouldn't need to sit down and meet face to face like some people do. Maybe you could just sent a note saying "I'm sorry for the pain and loss that I caused you. I'm not asking for your sympathy for where I am but just for your forgiveness."

If you would like to take the first step in doing this, here are some ideas that may be helpful.

SOME IDEAS AND SUGGESTIONS:

1) Allow someone else to help you. Talk it over with a chaplain or write to the addresses in the back of this book for information on victim offender reconciliation. A first step might be to contact your pastor or somebody else in your home community to see if they might be able to forward a letter to your victims. If that doesn't work, contact the local probation office and ask them to forward your letter. Or, maybe your parole office could help if you decide to do this after you get out.

2) The idea of offenders contacting their victims is pretty new and may cause some raised eyebrows when you suggest it because some communities have never heard of such a thing. The system is set up to keep you and the victim apart. That's why probation officers and other court persons may not be as helpful as they could be. They may even be somewhat suspicious of you and insist on reading any letters before forwarding them to the victims.

3) Be willing to accept one-way communication. Just because the victim doesn't respond doesn't mean that you have failed. It's possible your letter was not delivered—you might want to check that out. It's also possible that a victim is glad for your letter but doesn't know what to say. It's even possible that, because of your letter, you

may be forgiven months or years later. You may never know about it. Still, you have done your part by trying to make contact and should feel free to return to your community in peace.

4) Don't try to be heavy! Keep it simple. No one is asking you to put yourself down. Nor should you expect your victims to suddenly come to a totally new understanding of you. Your goal is simple restoration —just making right what was wrong.

5) If you have made a Christian commitment since you committed your crime, share that with your victim. Again, it can be as simple as ''I want you to know that God has forgiven me for what I did. I would also like to ask for your forgiveness.''

6) You may be in for the surprise of your life. It's possible that your victims may forgive you with words of encouragement and concern. They may even ask ''How can we help you?'' They may have lots of other questions, including ''Why did you do it?'' Sometimes miracles happen and offenders and their victims become real friends!

---

1. *Have you really forgiven yourself? Has God?*

2. *What if there was a financial loss—should you offer to pay restitution or do community service?*

3. *What if you contact your victims and they get angry because you're getting out already? Maybe they thought a five-year sentence meant you'd be gone five years.*

4. *Would it be better if your family also contacted them?*

KATHY: ''He sure got religion!''

''I guess I can live with it. It's not like I'm not a Christian. It's just, well, I don't see why you got to go overboard. No matter what I tell him he just says, 'O Honey, the Lord will take care of it.' Maybe he will, I don't know, but I can't see what it hurts to talk about it. The kids don't say much about it but I'm afraid it's going to cause problems. One week he says 'This is what the Lord wants'—the next week it's something else. I never know what to expect. Will it be like that when he gets home?''

THE PROBLEM:

Kathy is upset about her husband's religion. It's not because of *what* he believes—mostly she believes the same things. She's upset because of what he's *doing* with his new religious experience. Instead of sharing it with her and searching with her for what their faith might mean for their life together, he's coming to her with all the answers for both of them. He's like a religious lone ranger with a direct line from God. Because he personally gets his directions from God, Kathy is not supposed to question his ideas—that would be like questioning God. But it's impossible for her *not* to question when his vision of God's plan for them changes from week to week. Kathy just ends up wondering which preacher he's been listening to now.

Kathy wanted to plan for the future *with* her husband. She wanted them to share their ideas and beliefs while thinking about the things they will face when he comes home. But he won't talk *with* her, just *at* her. His faith is too self-centered to be able to listen to her so Kathy ends up feeling shut out—she doesn't know how he came to his present faith commitment or how he decided what to do about it. It seems his faith is just one more way for him to impose his ideas and values on her. Instead of drawing them together, it is pushing them apart.

SOME IDEAS AND SUGGESTIONS:

Decisions about how you relate to God are important. The awareness of God's care and presence is a real comfort to many people in prison. Some discover this comfort for the first time when they are in prison. For others, it's not a new experience.

Living with your faith can also create problems when others, particularly your family, don't seem to share it. Will you be tempted to give it all up in order to have peace in the family? Will you want to force them to see it your way? Here are some things to consider when you think of how you and your faith will fit in with family and friends who have not all had the same experiences you've had.

1) Don't assume that you are the only one who has heard from God. A new or a renewed faith commitment can be an exciting experience—it is something to celebrate and share with others. At the same time it is important to remember that your new faith beginning is just that—a beginning. Your early excitement may wear off. You may meet other believers who aren't very excited. But don't

let that fool you. Working out our faith means different things to different people. It may mean different things for you at different times. So when you talk about your beliefs, be ready to listen as well.

2) Try to find ways to work at your beliefs with other people, perhaps in a Bible study group or with a chaplain. Be willing to raise questions and to search; our faith ideas are best tested with other believers—they can help us judge whether our ideas are really from God or whether we are using God as a rubber stamp for our own ideas. We've all seen people like that—a guy whose religion is just another expression of his self-centeredness. He alone is right and everybody else is wrong. He sees no reason to be a part of a *body*—he is *it*. This kind of faith divides instead of unites. It weakens persons rather than strengthens them. It is a lonely faith.

3) Being right with God means we must also get right with people. It's not you and God *against* the rest of the world. To be sure, there is a personal side to our faith. We can't wait until everybody agrees with us, or sees it our way. Jesus didn't. But a Christian is not on a solo voyage. Although it may be hard for us to acknowledge at times, we all need other people, God's creation. The Christian voyage is meant to be shared—it is not meant for the same person to navigate day and night, without a break. Kathy wanted to share the navigating, she wanted to help steer the ship. Depending on God doesn't mean shutting others out the way Kathy was shut out by her husband. Depending on God means letting God come to us *through* other people. When we shut others out of our life and planning we may also be shutting God out.

4) Being a Christian does not give any of us the right to tell God what to do. Often when we pray we assume that we know the best answer to our request and it is easy to assume that God will do as we suggest. We are sometimes shocked then when God's answer is different from ours and we may be tempted to throw it all out the window. This problem really has nothing to do with your being in prison. *I* face the same thing and my neighbors face it too. Some people say that it is only at times like this, when God doesn't respond as we expect, that we find out if our faith (trust) is really in ourselves or in God.

---

1. *Can you and your family agree before you go home on which church to attend and how often you should go?*

2. *Are you using your dependence on God as a way of avoiding the responsibility of including others in your decisions?*

3. Are you able to take other people's views of God as seriously as your own? Or do you believe that you have some special understanding that no one else has?

A Closing Word

In some ways going home is a lot like getting married. No matter how much you think and plan ahead, you'll always run into something you're not quite ready for. That's why lots of couples today sit down with a pastor or a counselor before-hand to talk about what they should expect in marriage. It's not to discourage them but to give them a few extra tools to help make it work.

I hope that's what this booklet can be for you, a tool to help make things work for you. I didn't write it to discourage you. Rather, it is to help you get a handle on what's happening to you.

You may want to stick it in your sack and take it home. Read it again a few weeks after you get home. Maybe some things will make more sense after awhile. Or maybe you'll find that it makes even less sense.

I know I don't have the final word on what's happening to you—you know that better than anybody. Let me know if I've missed the boat here or there. You can also let me know what's most helpful for you. I'm still learning.

Peace,

Al Wengerd

Al Wengerd

Center for Community Justice
220 West High Street
Elkhart, Indiana 46516

AL WENGERD is Director of the Center for Community Justice in Elkhart, Indiana. He began his work with ex-prisoners following his graduation from Kent State University in 1972. For three years he was a counselor at a halfway house for men returning from prison. From 1975-1977, Al studied at the Associated Mennonite Biblical Seminaries, Elkhart, Indiana. He then returned to working with adults through the Elkhart Probation Department. In 1980 he resigned that position to work for the Mennonite church in prison ministries. This ministry involved him with prisoners and their families on a daily basis. In 1990, Al became director of the Center for Community Justice, a nonprofit organization operating programs such as the Victim-Offender Reconciliation Program.

This booklet is a reflection of Al's experience which is mostly with male prisoners. While the number of female prisoners is increasing steadily and this booklet may be helpful to them generally, it does not attempt to speak specifically to the many unique concerns faced by women in prison.

This booklet was developed jointly by the MCC U.S. Office of Criminal Justice and the Victim Offender Ministries Program of MCC Canada.

MCC U.S.   MCC Canada
Criminal Justice   Victim Offender Ministries
Box 500   P.O. Box 2038
Akron, Pennsylvania 17501-0500   Clearbrook, BC V2T 3T8

Many persons made helpful suggestions and comments on this project. I want to especially thank Ruby Friesen Zehr for all the hours she spent editing and rewriting several sections. Thanks also to those of you who are in prison who took the time to read the manuscript and send your evaluations. Lastly, without Howard Zehr's constant support and challenge to put in writing some of my observations and experiences, this booklet would have been only an idea.

Single copies of this booklet are available from one of the addresses above. Multiple copies (five or more) may be ordered by organizations at established discounts directly from the publisher: Herald Press, 616 Walnut Avenue, Scottdale, Pa. 15683, or Herald Press, 490 Dutton Drive, Waterloo, Ont. N2L 6H7.

You may also contact the organization listed below:

Related Books

Augsburger, David W. *Caring Enough to Confront.* Herald Press, 1980.
Augsburger, David W. *When Enough Is Enough: Discovering True Hope When All Hope Seems Lost.* Herald Press, 1984.
Zehr, Howard. *Changing Lenses: A New Focus for Crime and Justice.* Herald Press, 1995.